A Child's First Library of Learning

Dangerous Animals

TIME-LIFE BOOKS • ALEXANDRIA, VIRGINIA

Contents

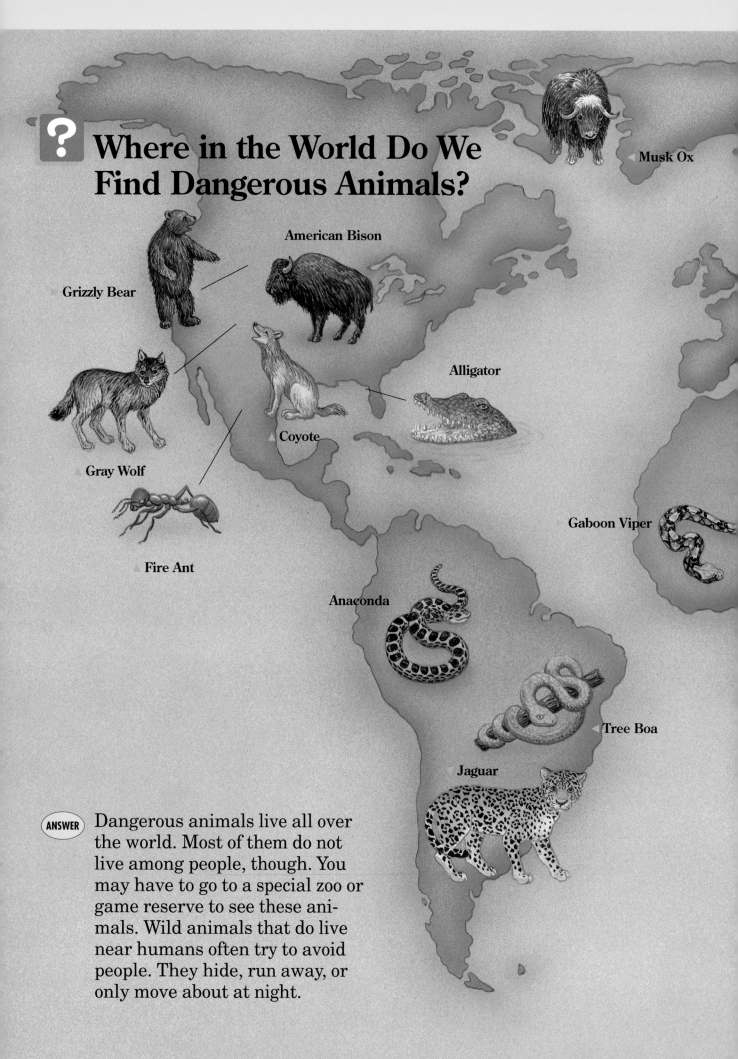

Where in the World Do We Find Dangerous Animals?

Musk Ox

American Bison

Grizzly Bear

Gray Wolf

Coyote

Alligator

Fire Ant

Gaboon Viper

Anaconda

Tree Boa

Jaguar

ANSWER Dangerous animals live all over the world. Most of them do not live among people, though. You may have to go to a special zoo or game reserve to see these animals. Wild animals that do live near humans often try to avoid people. They hide, run away, or only move about at night.

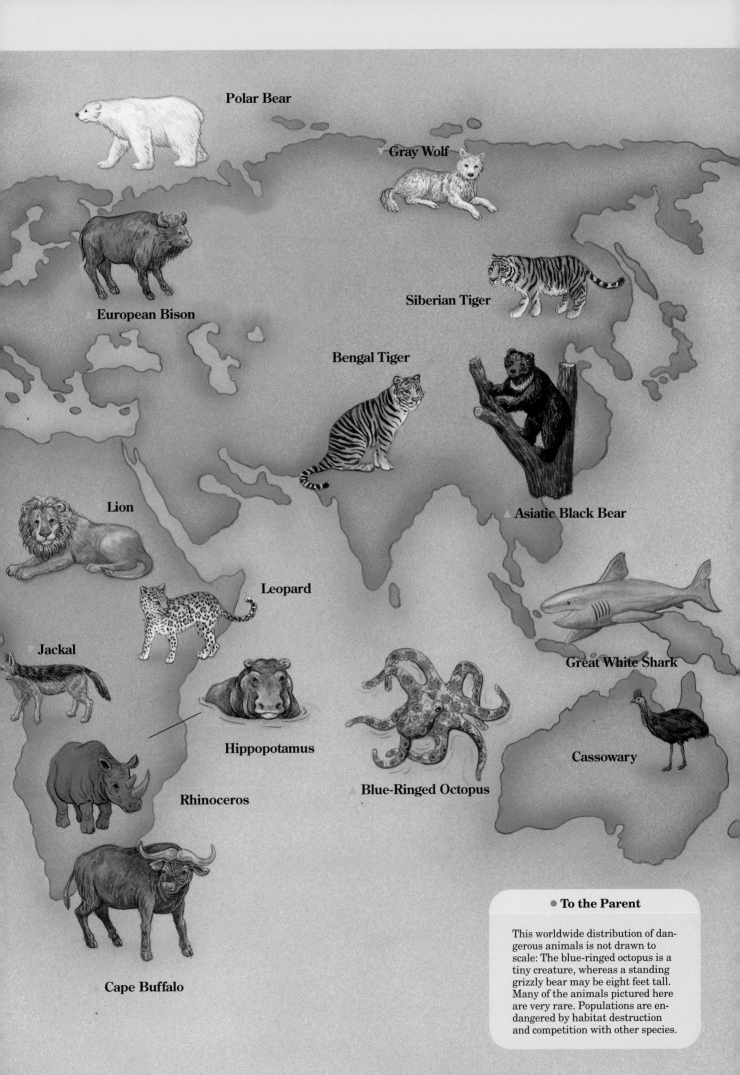

Polar Bear

Gray Wolf

European Bison

Siberian Tiger

Bengal Tiger

Asiatic Black Bear

Lion

Leopard

Great White Shark

Jackal

Hippopotamus

Rhinoceros

Blue-Ringed Octopus

Cassowary

Cape Buffalo

● To the Parent

This worldwide distribution of dangerous animals is not drawn to scale: The blue-ringed octopus is a tiny creature, whereas a standing grizzly bear may be eight feet tall. Many of the animals pictured here are very rare. Populations are endangered by habitat destruction and competition with other species.

? What Are an Animal's Weapons?

ANSWER Animals have evolved many ways of defending themselves and attacking others. Some use teeth and claws to hold and tear apart their food. Poisonous snakes use fangs to inject venom. Some insects sting. Hooves can keep an attacker away. Tusks and horns serve as tools for collecting food, but turn into weapons when needed.

▲ Hooves

◀ Teeth and jaws

▶ Fangs

▼ Tusks

▲ Stinger

▼ Antlers

▼ Horns

◀ Claws and teeth

6

Why do they attack?

Animals usually live peaceably and do not get mad or pick fights without reason. But there are some times when animals do attack each other. Then they fight until one animal gets away or is killed by the other. Unless they are hunting for food, most animals give warning signals before they attack.

▲ Defending territory

Many animals live within a personal territory where they graze or hunt and raise families. They mark out their territory and defend it from others.

▲ Courting and mating

At breeding time animals of the same kind may fight for rights to a desireable female. Strong, healthy males have the best chance to find a mate.

▲ Protecting the young

Females protecting their babies may attack without warning. They seem completely fearless and can drive off much larger animals in their fury.

▼ Hunger

When they are hungry, meat-eating animals hunt and attack other animals. Some hunt in groups, others alone.

● To the Parent

It is best to be wary of strange animals. Even pets can be dangerous if they feel threatened or have young ones. Danger signs include an animal's growl, a tensed body or raised fur, or an unwavering stare. In parks or wilderness areas always follow rangers' suggestions for observing wild animals safely.

Are There Any Dangerous Birds?

ANSWER Most birds don't look dangerous. They are smaller than humans, and they fly away if you go near them. But the cassowary, a bird that lives in Australia and New Guinea, can be a danger. Cassowaries are related to ostriches and emus. They stand more than five feet tall and cannot fly. Cassowaries have attacked and killed people who threatened their chicks.

■ **Crash helmet**

The bony crest on top of a cassowary's head works like a crash helmet. The crest helps protect the bird's head as it pushes through the undergrowth of the rainforest.

◀ Cassowaries use their big feet as weapons. When they attack, they slash their enemies with the daggerlike claws on their inner toes.

■ Swans and geese

Swans look peaceful gliding over the water, but they defend their mates and nests with vicious attacks. Angry swans will hiss and peck and beat their powerful wings at an intruder. They can break a man's ribs or arm. Geese are sometimes used as watchdogs. They stay alert at night, warn their owners with loud honking if a stranger comes, and attack by hissing and pecking.

MINI-DATA

10 ft

■ Big, bigger, biggest!

Ostriches are huge: The males can be up to eight feet tall and weigh 300 pounds. But *Aepyornis*, or elephant birds, were bigger. They once lived in Madagascar but became extinct long ago. Skeletons show they were over ten feet tall. One egg measured three feet around and weighed 26 pounds.

▲ **Ostriches**
Ostriches cannot fly, but they may kick to defend themselves. They don't hide their heads in sand either. It only looks that way from a distance.

● To the Parent

None of the largest birds, including ostriches, rheas, cassowaries, and emus, can fly. Their size, powerful legs, and running speed are their defenses. Other large birds that may look threatening, such as eagles and hawks, prey mostly on smaller birds, rodents, or fish. The big scavenger storks and vultures of Africa may challenge wild dogs or hyenas for possession of a kill, but they are wary of humans. One other bird, the pitohui of New Guinea, poses a danger: Its skin and feathers are poisonous *(see page 45)*.

How Do Elephants Use Their Tusks?

ANSWER Elephant tusks can be weapons, or they can be handy tools. When two bulls fight for mates, one may threaten another by showing his tusks or swing the tusks to jab the other in the side. Most of the time, elephants use their tusks for getting food or water. They uproot the shrubs and trees they eat by pressing the tusks against them, then pulling the shrubs up with their trunk.

■ Ivory weapons

Fighting elephants sometimes lock their tusks together and thrash back and forth. They keep on wrestling as each tries to break the tusks of the other.

■ Digging tools

Elephants need salt in their diet. They dig salt out of rock or clay with their tusks. Sometimes they dig for water in places where water has gone underground. Each elephant uses one tusk the most in the same way you use your right or left hand the most.

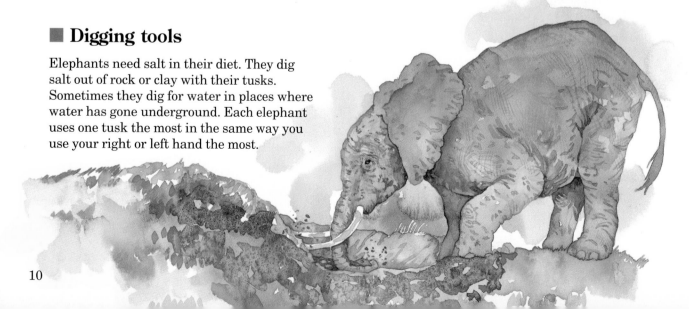

Levers and lifters

Elephants use their tusks most often as levers to pry up young trees or as lifters to carry logs. Both male and female elephants grow tusks, which are really specialized teeth. Tusks grow about seven inches a year. Elephants like to rest with their trunks draped over the tusks.

▲ Terrific tusks

The longest tusks on record belonged to Ahmed, an elephant from Kenya. His tusks were ten feet long and weighed 148 pounds each. A statue in Ahmed's honor has been erected at the National Museum in Kenya's capital of Nairobi.

CHECK IT OUT

■ Natural snorkels

Elephants have fun in the water. They can walk or swim underwater. Holding their trunks above the water, they breathe through their trunks like divers using snorkels.

11

Why Does a Rhinoceros Charge?

ANSWER A rhinoceros stands between five and six feet tall and weighs up to three tons--more than a large car--so most creatures don't bother it. But when someone crosses its path, a rhino will get mad. Female rhinos charge at any danger that may threaten their calves—even lions or people. Male rhinos mark out large personal territories and charge at other rhino intruders. A charging rhino may run at 30 miles an hour for a short distance.

■ Trailblazer's rights

Rhinos in India and Southeast Asia make trails through the grassy jungles where they live. They defend the trails by charging at anyone who uses them. But anyone near, not on, the trail is safe.

■ What's the difference?

Wild rhinoceroses live only in Africa and Asia. Both the black and white rhino species are African, and both are grayish in color, but the white rhinos are larger and have longer horns. Some Asian rhinos are covered with thin, coarse hair.

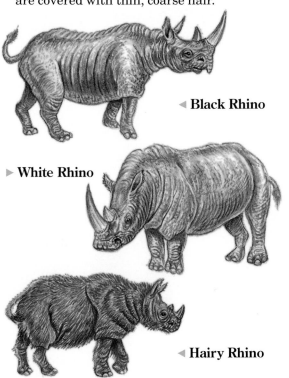

◄ **Black Rhino**

► **White Rhino**

◄ **Hairy Rhino**

▼ Horned combat

Sometimes rhino charges do not end an argument, and the rhinos fight seriously. They may push at each other with their heads, try to stab with their horns, or bite with their sharp front teeth.

● To the Parent

The rhinoceros family is an ancient one: Woolly rhinos roamed across Europe and America during the Ice Ages. Today's endangered rhinos live in Africa, India, and the jungles of Southeast Asia. Rhinos are vegetarian browsers, eating grass, leaves, and twigs. Indian and Javan rhinos have a single horn; other species have two. Horns are made of dense, hair-like fibers. They grow longer as the animals mature. Poachers kill rhinos for their horns, which are used in Asian medicines and as ornamental dagger hilts.

Why Do Buffaloes Stampede?

(ANSWER) Buffaloes stampede when they are surprised or frightened. They run in a wild, headlong rush, which works as a defense. The big mass of racing animals may trample the predator that threatens them. The predator could be a human or an animal hunter. The running herd raises dust, making it hard for predators to see and helping the buffaloes escape. Many other hoofed animals stampede, including the antelope, gnu, and zebra.

■ What is a predator?

A predator is an animal that lives by killing and eating other animals. The animal that is chased by the predator is called the prey.

■ Wet and wonderful

Water holes are not just for drinking. The Cape Buffalo of Africa also love to wallow in the water and the mud. Buffalo and bison are relatives of cattle.

What is a bison?

Bison are related to buffalo, but their body shape, horns, and number of ribs are different. Bison live in Europe and in North America, where they are often called buffalo. Real buffalo live only in Africa, India, and Southeast Asia.

▲ **European Bison**

European bison eat grass, leaves, and twigs. They live in the forests of Poland, in Eastern Europe, and in zoos.

▲ **American Bison**

American bison eat only grass. They live on the open prairie in the United States and Canada. Their heads and shoulders are heavier than the European bison's.

■ Defensive circle

Buffalo and musk oxen, like those shown below, sometimes protect their calves from other dangerous animals by forming a ring of adults around them. Predators cannot get through that circle of horns to attack the young ones.

● **To the Parent**

African buffalo have strong protective instincts. They may even come to the rescue of other animals from their herd who are under attack by predators. Buffalo herds in Africa and bison herds in North America are slowly growing again after many years of being endangered by hunters and deadly diseases.

15

Why Do Lions Hunt in Groups?

ANSWER Most lions live in family groups of female lions, cubs, and two or three male lions. The lionesses do most of the hunting. Working as a team they can catch more prey than each working alone. When lionesses make a kill, the rest of the family comes to eat.

▼ A female lion and two cubs are waiting for prey.

▼ 1. In a typical hunt, female lions check out the situation first. Here they have spotted a likely meal: gazelles at a water hole. Though the lionesses get ready for action, they stay hidden among the trees until the last minute.

▲ 2. When the gazelles begin to leave, the lionesses move rapidly to surround their prey. Arrows show how they run. The hunting lionesses split up so they can cover different escape routes from the water hole. Seeing lions all around helps to confuse the gazelles.

▲ 4. When one lioness makes a kill, the other females, males, and young ones of her family come to share the meal. Usually the males eat first, then the adult lionesses, and the cubs come last of all.

▲ 3. As the gazelles scatter and run for cover, a lioness gets close to one. She can run very fast for a short distance. When she is near, she pounces, pulls the gazelle down, and bites its throat till the animal dies.

▲ Zebras are a favorite food of lions. A mighty bound will bring this zebra down.

■ What is a carnivore?

A carnivore is an animal that eats the flesh of another animal. Among the carnivores are insects, birds, reptiles, amphibians, and mammals. Most carnivores have to hunt to catch their food. Some carnivores also eat plants; those are called omnivores, meaning they will eat everything.

Why Do Tigers Hunt at Night?

ANSWER Tigers are the largest of all cats. They live and hunt alone. Because they move slowly, they must get close to a prey animal to catch it. So they lie in tall grass or bushes at night, waiting for prey near a water hole. When animals come to drink, the tiger can leap out of its hiding place to attack them with its sharp claws and strong jaws.

▲ **Bengal Tiger**
These tigers live in India, Southeast Asia, and parts of China. There are no tigers in Africa. Female tigers are much smaller than males.

▲ **Siberian Tiger**
These are the largest tigers, growing up to nine feet long and weighing more than 600 pounds.

Can a tiger purr?

The big cats—tigers, leopards, and li-ons—cannot purr, although they make a powerful roar. Small cats, like our house pets, wildcats, and cougars, purr by vibrating two bones at the base of their tongues. The bones are shaped differently in the throats of the bigger cats, and they don't vibrate.

MINI-DATA

■ Anti man-eater masks

Since tigers prefer to attack from the rear, forest workers in northern India protect themselves by wearing face masks on the back of their head. The tigers do not come near if they think a man is facing them. Man-eating tigers are rare. They are usually too old or too weak to hunt wild prey, and their territo-ry has been invaded by human workers.

▲ **White Tiger**
Sometimes normal colored tigers give birth to cubs that are white with black stripes. These rare animals are treasured by zoos and other owners.

● To the Parent

Centuries of intensive trophy hunt-ing have endangered both the Ben-gal and the Siberian tigers. Recent attempts to protect them may save the tigers from extinction. Males and females mate, then go their separate ways. The female raises three or four cubs, teaching them hunting skills. Tigers enjoy water and swim or lounge in rivers.

? How Does a Leopard Stalk Its Prey?

ANSWER Leopards are experts at using cover to help them hunt. A hungry leopard gets close to its prey by creeping through tall grasses or crouching behind bushes or rocks. One leopard was seen using a photographer's truck to hide behind. When a leopard is close to its victim, it springs to kill in one or two quick leaps.

A surprise attack
Leopards and other hunting cats take advantage of times when their prey is drinking. The antelopes above cannot look for predators and drink at the same time. Drinking animals are also slower getting away if their hooves slip or stick in the mud.

■ Leopard storage lockers

Leopards are the best tree climbers of the great cats. They leap from trees onto prey animals. They also use trees to store the animals they have killed until they are ready to eat. Because they can save their meat and do not share, leopards do not need to kill as often as some predators do.

MINI-DATA

■ Black panthers

Most leopards are tan with black spots, but a few leopards have black fur marked with black spots; they are called black panthers.

● **To the Parent**

Noted for their boldness, leopards have been found living close to large African cities. In spite of this adaptation, leopards are endangered. They are hunted because they prey on domestic animals and for their beautiful coats. Indian leopards living near forest villages may become man-eaters when small children make tempting prey at night.

Why Does a Jaguar Follow Its Prey into the Water?

ANSWER Jaguars often hunt near water in the forests where they live. A jaguar may leap on its prey when water slows it down, making the chase easier. Jaguars like to eat turtles, ducks, and other water animals. They crouch at the edge of a river and scoop fish up with their paws. Larger prey, like the water hog at right, can be found at the water's edge.

22

How can you tell a jaguar from a leopard?

Jaguars live only in Central and South America. Leopards live on different continents, in Africa and Asia. Jaguars are larger than leopards and are not as swift in trees. Both jaguars and leopards are tan or black with black-ringed markings. What makes the jaguar's fur different are the smaller black dots within the rings of the dark markings.

■ **Jaguar**   ■ **Leopard**

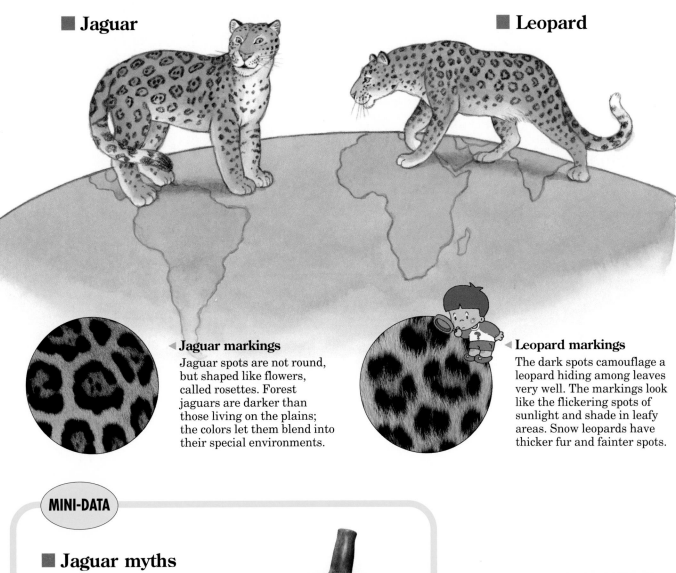

◀ **Jaguar markings**
Jaguar spots are not round, but shaped like flowers, called rosettes. Forest jaguars are darker than those living on the plains; the colors let them blend into their special environments.

◀ **Leopard markings**
The dark spots camouflage a leopard hiding among leaves very well. The markings look like the flickering spots of sunlight and shade in leafy areas. Snow leopards have thicker fur and fainter spots.

MINI-DATA

■ **Jaguar myths**

For centuries the people of Central and South America honored the jaguar for its strength and beauty as a god. They made statues and pottery in the shape of a jaguar, such as the pot at right from the Moche culture of ancient Peru.

● **To the Parent**

The jaguar is the largest cat found in the Americas. It does not roar, but makes coughing, grunting noises. Jaguars have sharp, strong fangs that pierce the skulls of their victims, making kills easy to document. The spread of human settlements and the demand for jaguars' spotted coats has severely reduced the number of these big cats.

Why Do Wolves Travel in Packs?

ANSWER Wolves form packs because working together is easier than working alone. A pack of wolves can kill large animals like moose or caribou. Wolf cubs are well cared for by many babysitters, and the adults bring them plenty of food. Wolves carefully patrol their home territory and defend it against other packs. But sometimes an adult leaves the group and lives as a lone wolf.

With the leader in front and lined up in hunting formation, these wolves follow in each other's tracks searching for prey. When they close in on a prey animal and the prey is exhausted, they circle in for the kill.

Who's who in a wolf pack?

Wolf packs are ruled by a strong adult male, called the alpha wolf. He and his mate are the only parents in the pack. Younger adults follow the alpha wolf's lead in the hunt. They show their obedience by cowering and licking the alpha wolf's face, and they allow him to eat first at a kill. Wolf cubs play a lot and develop strong ties with the other pack members.

■ At a wolf den

Between seven and 20 wolves are in a pack. Five or six cubs are born each year in a den among rocks or in burrows dug by the parents. Some pack adults stay with the cubs while others hunt and bring them food. When the cubs are old enough to run, they join the pack in hunting.

● To the Parent

Cooperative behavior among wolves may have evolved during the Ice Age, when prey animals were large and hunts needed more participants. Today wolves live mostly in the Arctic regions; they have been driven away from human settlements. In spite of legends of savage wolf attacks, modern research indicates wolves are not a danger to humans.

❓ **Why Does the Coyote Howl?**

(ANSWER) The coyotes of North America are the noisiest animals in the dog family. They howl to tell members of their clan where they are. They howl when they make a kill. They howl to tell strange coyotes to stay away from their territory. Some scientists think they even howl because they like the sound. Coyotes also growl, yelp, whine, and bark. All coyotes understand the same sounds. They can howl up a musical scale of two octaves.

■ **Wily coyotes**

Coyotes are smart creatures. They can survive wherever they find food. Although they are animals of the prairies, some live in cities today. They will eat mice, fruit, insects, and even pizza crusts from over-turned garbage cans.

What are some of the coyote's relatives?

The jackal is a close cousin of the coyote. Jackals are about the same size, and they also live by hunting and scavenging. They roam through Africa, Asia, and parts of Europe.

The African Hunting Dog lives in large family packs on the plains. Their odd-colored coats serve as camouflage to help hide them, but make them look more like hyenas than dogs.

▼ **Jackal**

▲ **African Hunting Dog**

■ The pounce

◀ Coyotes listen carefully as they hunt. When they hear a mouse scurrying in the grass, they wait for just the right moment before they pounce on it. Coyotes also prey on animals as large as deer.

▲ This looks like a good bite for lunch.

What Do Hyenas Laugh About?

ANSWER Africa's spotted hyenas laugh when they are excited. They yelp and growl and make other loud noises that sound like laughing after they kill their prey. This laughter tells the other hyenas of the clan that it is time to eat. The brown and striped hyena species of Africa are not as noisy as the spotted ones.

▲ Hyenas aren't laughing because they think something is funny. They use the sound as a signal to others.

▼ Hyena laughter does not only alert other hyenas. Lions often come as well, when they hear the hyenas, and demand a share of the food. In some areas, half of what lions eat is taken from the hyenas.

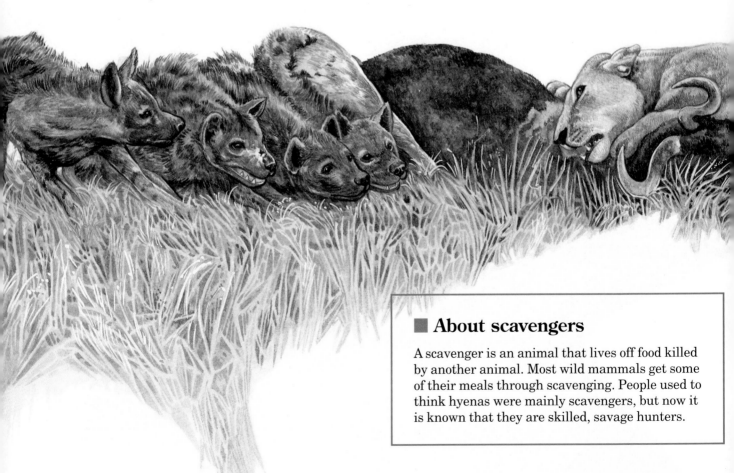

■ About scavengers

A scavenger is an animal that lives off food killed by another animal. Most wild mammals get some of their meals through scavenging. People used to think hyenas were mainly scavengers, but now it is known that they are skilled, savage hunters.

■ Large clans

Spotted hyenas live in family groups called clans. A clan may have up to 80 hyenas who defend their territory and often hunt together. Hyenas chase some large prey, including antelope and young rhinoceros. Even baby hyenas are dangerous. Sometimes newborn cubs attack each other.

■ Rule by mothers

The head of a hyena clan is the "matriarch," an adult female. The females are larger and feared by the males. Their cubs are born as twins.

● **To the Parent**

Hyenas are the most abundant carnivores in Africa. Clans patrol their established territories tirelessly, and hunt day and night. They prey on anything from small rodents to young rhinos. Though they look a lot like dogs, hyenas are more closely related to cats. Hyenas have killed children and isolated humans in Africa and India.

? Can a Polar Bear Fight a Walrus?

ANSWER Polar bears are the largest bears in the world. They are the biggest meat-eaters on land anywhere. Male polar bears can weigh up to 1,700 pounds and measure eight feet at the shoulder when they rear up on their hind legs. They live along the edge of the arctic ice, where they eat mainly seals. Sometimes, though, they will fight with a young walrus and kill it to eat.

▶ **Patient hunters**

The big white bears catch their usual food—seals—by "still hunting." This means they find a hole in the ice where a seal will come up to breathe. Then they lie down to wait. Sometimes they wait for hours without moving. When they hear the seal coming through the hole, they pounce on it. This kind of hunting helps the bears conserve energy.

■ Strong walkers

Polar bears walk for many miles looking for food. When summer comes, they may go to grassy places to eat berries. In the winter, they travel with the ice across the Arctic Ocean. Some bears have a hunting area that covers more than 77,000 square miles. It would take you about 55 days just to walk around the edges of it.

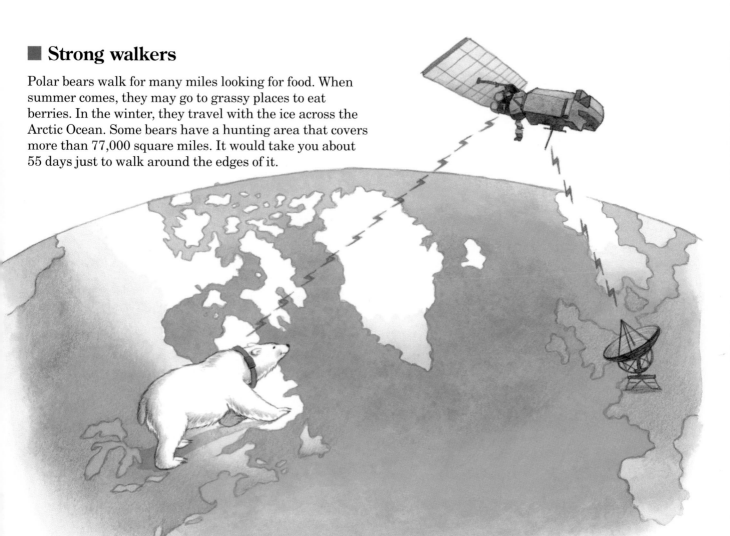

MINI-DATA

■ Polar bears are black

Under their thick white fur, polar bears have black skin. The black skin helps them stay warm. Heat from the sun travels down their hollow hairs. When the heat reaches the skin, the black color helps to hold it in. You can see the black skin on the bottoms of their paws and on their noses.

▲ Eyes in the sky

Scientists follow polar bears by satellite. To track them, scientists put a radio collar on a bear's neck, and the collar sends signals to a satellite. The satellite then sends the signals to a receiver in France. There, a computer draws a map of the bear's travels.

● To the Parent

Polar bears are solitary, nomadic animals that live almost exclusively on seals, except in a few areas, such as Churchill on the Hudson Bay in Canada, where they have learned to eat garbage. Although they can be dangerous if provoked, they very rarely attack humans, and, in fact, have dwindled greatly in number due to human hunters.

How Should You Watch a Grizzly Bear?

ANSWER Although grizzly bears hardly ever attack people, you should still be careful when you're in grizzly country. These 1,000-pound brown bears live mainly in the mountains of western North America. They like to eat fruit, honey, fish, and small animals. Grizzlies can be dangerous if they are surprised. If you see one, you should watch it from far away and not bother it.

■ Five rules for grizzly country

If you are hiking or camping where grizzlies live, you should first talk to park rangers about how to behave around bears.

Here are some basic rules that most rangers will tell you.

1 No surprises: Bears don't like surprises. Let them know you are coming. Make noise—whistle, sing, talk loudly. Wear a bell on your backpack.

2 Stay far away: If you suddenly see a bear, don't try to get any closer. Stay at least 300 feet away—about the length of football field.

3 **No food:** When camping, store food far from your tent. Try hanging it from a rope hung from a tree. Wash dishes far from camp, and don't wear food-stained clothes.

4 **Don't run:** Don't run when you see a bear. Bears are much faster than you are. Wait quietly until the bear leaves, or walk away slowly, staying upwind so the bear can smell you.

5 **Climb a tree:** If a grizzly is close and charges, try to climb a tree—but only if you can get about 10 feet up. Otherwise, curl up in a ball on the ground.

■ What about black bears?

Black bears are less dangerous than grizzlies. Still, the same rules apply, except for climbing trees. Black bears are good climbers. Curl up on the ground if one comes close.

● **To the Parent**

The grizzly bear is a variety of brown bear marked by silver-tipped fur, and a bent, "Roman" nose. Grizzlies are found mainly in the Rocky Mountains of the western United States and Canada and in Alaska. Grizzly attacks—like the bears themselves—are rare. Nevertheless, if a bear is surprised at close range, and if it has cubs or a fresh kill, it might charge. When visiting any area known to have grizzlies, check with park rangers first and learn their rules.

Does a Moose Use Its Antlers as a Weapon?

ANSWER The big, sweeping antlers on a male moose's head look dangerous. But the moose uses its antlers mainly to shove around other moose. This seven-foot-tall, 1,400-pound animal is the largest member of the deer family. Moose live mainly in the forests of northern North America. In the fall, male, or "bull," moose will lower their heads and butt each other with their antlers. The stronger moose will get to go off with a female. The weaker one will walk away.

▲ Two bull moose wrestle with their antlers.

■ New antlers every year

Bull moose grow a new set of antlers each year. (Females don't have antlers.) The antlers are made of bone. They start growing in the spring and drop off in the winter. Each year the antlers get bigger.

▲ Two years old   ▲ Four years old   ▲ Eight years old

■ Wolves beware

When moose are attacked by their enemies, such as wolves or bears, they fight back with their feet. Moose have sharp hooves. One good kick from a big moose can kill a wolf.

■ A huge spread

Moose grow the largest antlers in the animal world. A grown moose, about ten years old, can have antlers that spread more than seven feet—as wide as a basketball player is tall.

■ Antlers all around

▲ **Whitetail Deer**

▲ **Reindeer**

Almost all deer, such as the whitetail deer and the reindeer above, have antlers of some kind. Some have little prongs. Others have huge racks that look like giant outspread hands. In most kinds of deer, only the male has antlers. The exception is the reindeer: Both the male and female have these bony headdresses.

Is the Tasmanian Devil Dangerous?

ANSWER The Tasmanian devil is noisy, smelly, and bad-tempered, but it is not dangerous to people. The little devil lives on the island of Tasmania off the coast of Australia. It is about two or three feet long—only as big as a small dog. Like many Australian mammals, it is a marsupial. This means the female carries her babies in a pouch on her belly.

■ Temper, temper

The cartoon Taz and the real Tasmanian devil have a few things in common. They both have bad tempers and whirl back and forth. When real Tasmanian devils are fighting, they jump from side to side so fast that they are hard to see.

■ Little devils, big eaters

Tasmanian devils love to eat, and they are not picky about their dinner. Sometimes they eat many times their own weight in food. One devil, after escaping from captivity, ate 54 chickens in two days.

■ Loudmouths

Visitors to Tasmania can hear the devils from miles away. They have a loud, eerie, whining growl that is sometimes followed by a snarling cough.

● **To the Parent**

The Tasmanian devil was once widespread on the continent of Australia, but since dingos have taken over much of the countryside, it is now found only on the island of Tasmania. Although it is hot-tempered and noisy in the wild, the devil is said to make a good pet, fond of washing in clean water and basking in the sun.

Does a Vampire Bat Really Suck Blood?

ANSWER Vampire bats don't suck blood—but they drink the blood of some large animals. These bats of Central and South America fly at night. When they find dinner—perhaps a sleep- ing cow or a horse—they land on it. With their razor-sharp teeth, they bite the animal and lick up a little of its blood. The bite is so painless that the animal does not wake up.

Bats fly swiftly through the night, reaching speeds of nearly 60 miles per hour. Their great wings are really arms and hands with long fingers that are covered with a tough skin. They flap their wings like swimmers use their arms doing the butterfly stroke. In search of food, they patrol an area of up to eight square miles.

■ Hop to it

Most bats launch themselves into flight from a tree or the roof of a cave. But vampire bats can take off from the ground. They use their claw-like thumbs and legs to walk or hop around and lift themselves up to get airborne.

▲ 1. A vampire bat prepares for takeoff.

▲ 3. A final push with its thumb propels the bat into the air.

▲ 2. With a skip and a jump, and a hop and a leap, the bat bounces along the ground, pushing off with its powerful legs.

▲ 4.Once in the air—at least six inches above the ground—the bat can spread its wings and fly.

MINI-DATA

Vampire dinner

A vampire bat may lap up more than its own weight in blood. (It only weighs about one ounce.) If the bat drinks for a long time, its stomach swells until the vampire looks like a little ball. Sometimes vampire bats drink so much blood that they get too full to fly.

● **To the Parent**

The range of the vampire bat extends from northern Mexico into southern South America. Although a bat will occasionally bite a sleeping human, it poses no threat to people from blood loss. The real danger from this mammal—as with other wild animals—lies in the transmission of rabies.

Are There Real Dragons?

 ANSWER Stories about fire-breathing dragons have been around for thousands of years. No one today has ever seen a dragon like those. The closest thing in the natural world to a fairy-tale dragon is the Komodo dragon of Indonesia. This huge lizard even has a yellow tongue that looks like flickering fire.

■ The biggest dragon

The largest living lizard, the Komodo dragon, grows up to ten feet long—as long as two bicycles put together—and can weigh 300 pounds.

■ Island dragons

With their long, powerful tail and sawlike teeth, Komodo dragons look pretty scary. They eat dead animals and live ones, such as deer and pigs. The dragons are named for the largest of the islands they live on—Komodo, near Java in Indonesia.

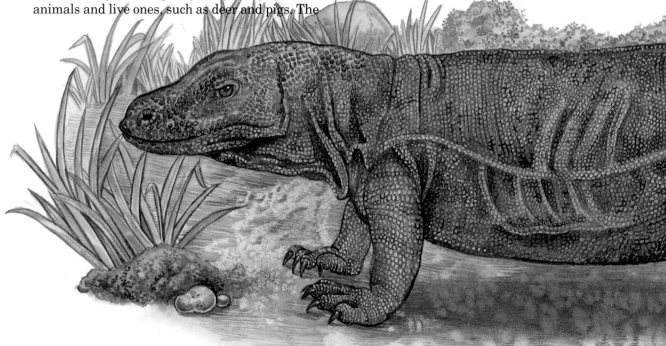

■ Other dragons

◀ Bearded Dragon

The bearded dragon, an Australian lizard, lives in hot, dry places. When it feels threatened, or wants to attract a female, it puffs out its spiny throat pouch—which makes it look like a beard—and opens its mouth wide to show the yellow inside.

◀ Water Dragon

Water dragons, found in Australia and Asia, are not really dragons, although they do have a long, drag-onlike crest down their backs. They are two- or three-foot-long lizards that can swim well.

● To the Parent

Komodo dragons, long known to Indonesians, were discovered by Westerners only in 1912. These huge carrion eaters rarely attack humans, but powerful bacteria in their saliva make their bites toxic. Because of the limited range and small numbers of breeding pairs, they are endangered.

What's the Difference between an Alligator and a Crocodile?

ANSWER Alligators and crocodiles are reptiles that look a lot alike. You can tell them apart by their teeth and the shape of their heads. Crocodiles have a big lower tooth on each side of their jaws that sticks up when their mouths are closed. The crocodile's head is longer and skinnier than the alligator's.

▲ **Crocodile**

▲ **Alligator**

■ A sudden lunge

▲ When they are not hunting, alligators spend hours lying on the banks of rivers and water holes, warming themselves in the sun.

▲ After a while, an alligator gets hungry. If it sees some likely prey—such as a bird, a frog, or a turtle—it gets up on its short legs and walks quietly into the water.

► Suddenly, the alligator lunges. Moving at lightning speed, the animal can shoot its whole body up out of the water to snatch its victim.

42

Can alligators live in sewers?

Before alligators were protected by law, people used to buy the babies as pets. Sadly, some of these little reptiles got flushed down the toilet when their owners couldn't take care of them. This gave rise to stories that alligators were living and growing in the sewers of big cities such as New York and Miami. These stories were completely untrue. Alligators have never lived in the sewers, but people liked to believe this anyway.

■ Alligator moms

Alligators are careful mothers. When the babies hatch from eggs, the mother will pick up each one gently in her mouth. Then she will carry it to the water and take care of it while it is small.

● **To the Parent**

Alligators and crocodiles are related. Alligators and their close relatives the caimans are found only in the Americas and China; crocodiles are more widespread, living in both fresh and salt water in Africa, Australia, Asia, the southernmost United States, and Central and South America. Both animals are threatened from loss of habitat and from hunting for their skins.

How Do Animals Use Venom?

ANSWER Animals have many ways of using the poisonous liquid called venom to stop an attacker. Some animals bite and others sting; some have venomous barbs and others spit the venom through the air. Most venomous animals do not have enough venom to hurt people. A few, though, are very dangerous.

▶ **Barbs**
Some fish, such as the lionfish, have venomous barbs sticking up from their backs. These can cause great pain and even kill an unlucky person who steps on them.

◀ **Tentacles**
The tentacles that float under most jellyfish have stinging cells in them. The cells shoot out venomous threads when they are touched.

▲ **Stinger**
Scorpions and some insects, such as ants and bees, have stingers on the ends of their bodies. These needle-sharp points inject venom.

▲ **Fangs**
Venomous snakes, such as this rattlesnake, and spiders have fangs—special hollow or grooved teeth that carry the poison.

■ Most poisonous

It is hard to say which animal is the most venomous in the world. Scientists don't know enough about all of them yet. Still, the animals at right are, drop for drop of venom, among the most dangerous anywhere. Any one of them can quickly kill a human being.

▲ **Blue-Ringed Octopus**

▲ **Poison-Arrow Frog**

▲ **Stonefish**

▲ Skin

Many amphibians, such as frogs and toads, can release poison through their skin if something threatens them or if they are handled roughly.

▲ Feathers

At least one bird species—the pitohui of Papua New Guinea—has poisonous feathers and skin.

▲ Spurs

The male duck-billed platypus has not only webbed feet and a rubbery bill, but also sharp venomous spurs on its hind legs.

▲ Spray

The spitting cobra does just that—it spits venom through openings in its fangs, aiming for an attacker's eyes.

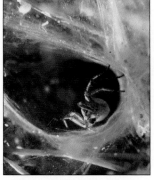

▲ Funnel-Web Spider

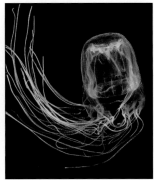

▲ Sea Wasp Jellyfish

How Does the Gila Monster Kill Its Prey?

ANSWER The gila monster is not very monsterlike. It is a slow, fat lizard that lives in the deserts of the American southwest. Eggs and small mammals, such as mice, are its favorite foods. The gila monster gets its scary name from the fact that it has a venomous bite. But it rarely ever harms people.

▲ The gila monster's brightly colored skin and calm nature make it a popular pet.

■ Lizard trackers

Gila monsters track down their food with smell rather than sight. Using their tongues to pick up the scent of birds or mice, the lizards can follow a trail for a long way.

■ Don't poke a gila monster in the mouth

▲ Beaded Lizard

The beaded lizard is the only other venomous lizard in the world. This lizard is a close relative of the gila monster and lives mainly in Mexico.

◄ Unlike other venomous reptiles, the gila monster has no fangs. Its venom is part of its saliva. When a gila monster bites down, it chews on its victim slowly, delivering venom into the wound.

MINI-DATA

■ Monster myths

Many wild stories have been told about the mild-mannered gila monster. People in the Southwest used to say that it would leap on its enemies, that it had evil-smelling breath, or that it could spit venom. Some even claimed that it had magical powers and could live forever.

● **To the Parent**

The gila (hee-la) monster takes its name from the Gila River system in southwest Arizona. Although it is venomous, its poison would only kill a human if it bit the person many times. The placid lizard is a popular exhibit in small zoos, so much so that its numbers in the wild are now greatly reduced.

47

How Do Vipers Use Their Fangs?

ANSWER Vipers are a large group of venomous snakes. Rattlesnakes, puff adders, and bushmasters are vipers. They use their long curved fangs to bite and get poisonous venom into the bloodstream of their victims. These fangs are special front teeth that are hollow or grooved so that venom flows through them.

▲ As a viper gets ready to strike, it tilts its head back and opens its jaws. The fangs spring forward, ready for the viper to bite. When they are not in use, the fangs fold back into a kind of pocket.

What are the two kinds of vipers?

Vipers are divided into two groups—pit vipers and true vipers. Pit vipers have a "pit" between their nose and eyes. This is a special organ that feels heat. The snake uses the pit to find warm prey, such as birds and mice. It can track a warm animal even in the dark.

▶ **Pit Viper**

The pit viper at right is a rattlesnake with a pit on either side of its head. Other pit vipers are the copperhead, bushmaster, and water moccasin.

▼ **True viper**

The Gaboon viper, below, and the puff adder are true vipers. They do not have a heat-sensing pit.

Which Is the Most Poisonous Snake?

ANSWER Sea snakes are the most dangerous of all venomous reptiles. These little-known cousins of cobras live in the warm waters of the Pacific and Indian Oceans. They spend their lives swimming in the sea and eating fish. They rarely bite people—but when they do, the person can die within a few hours.

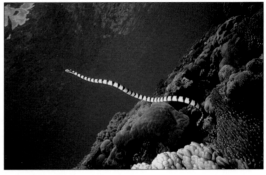

▲ A black-headed sea snake is ready to strike.

▶ Fishermen in the Pacific often pull up sea snakes in their fish nets. Sometimes they haul up as many as 100 at one time. The fishermen usually take the snakes out by hand and toss them back into the water. The snakes almost never bite.

■ **One deadly drop**

Sea snake venom is so deadly that one tiny drop, smaller than a teardrop, could kill three adults.

Can it move on water and land?

Sea snakes have just the right shape for life in the ocean.
Their bodies are flattened and have a tail like a paddle.
Their nostrils are on top of their heads. Inside, they have
a long lung that runs the length of their body. With one
breath, they can stay underwater for hours.

◄ **Not built for land**

Most sea snakes are helpless on land.
Unlike land snakes, they do not have large,
flat scales under the bodies to help them
crawl on the ground. Their flat, up-and-
down bodies are good only for swimming.

▲ **Narrow, flattened body**

Paddlelike tail

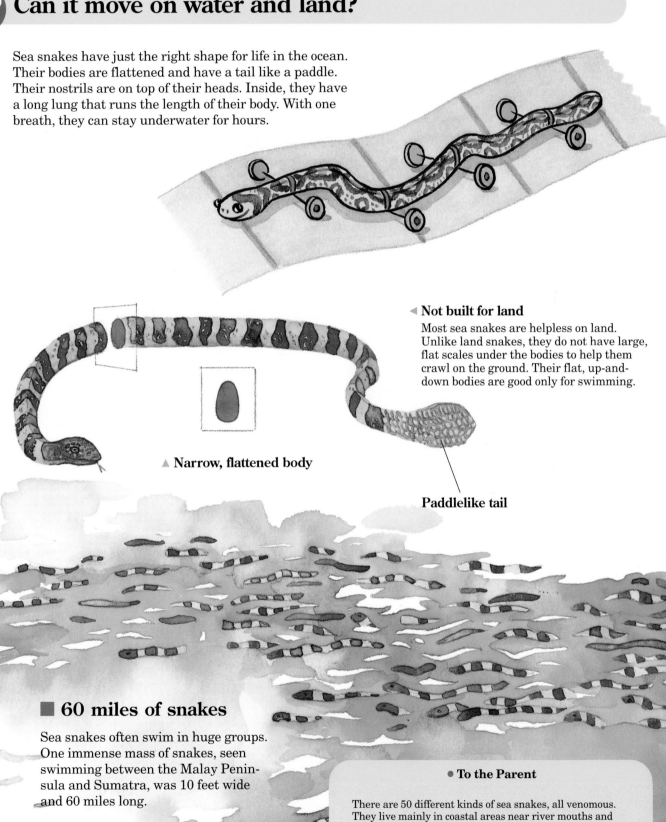

■ **60 miles of snakes**

Sea snakes often swim in huge groups.
One immense mass of snakes, seen
swimming between the Malay Penin-
sula and Sumatra, was 10 feet wide
and 60 miles long.

● **To the Parent**

There are 50 different kinds of sea snakes, all venomous.
They live mainly in coastal areas near river mouths and
bays, so they are often met by fishers and divers. Sea snake
venom is a neurotoxin—immediately after the bite, there is
little reaction, but gradually the victim becomes paralyzed
and, if not treated, will die of heart failure.

51

Do Cobras Really Dance to Music?

ANSWER In India, there are men called snake charmers. They play a flute, swaying back and forth. In front of them—but out of striking distance—a deadly cobra seems to dance to the music. The cobra is not really dancing, though. It cannot even hear the music, because snakes are deaf. The cobra is just following the man's movements. As the snake charmer sways, the snake sways too, trying to watch him.

■ The dance of love

Even though cobras do not dance for snake charmers, they do dance for each other. If a male and female are attracted to one another, they may "dance" for an hour or more, weaving their long, upright bodies back and forth.

Why does the cobra spread its hood?

Cobras are famous for their hoods. When they are threatened or excited, the snakes lift their heads from the ground and spread out long rib bones. The ribs pull loose skin out into a hood that warns "Stay away, or I'll bite!" In some cobras, the hood is rather small. In the Indian cobra, the hood is wide and marked by a pattern that looks like a pair of eyeglasses. The patterned hood gives the snake the nickname of spectacled cobra.

▲ When cobras feel threatened, they rear up, hiss, and spread their hoods to frighten away their attacker.

■ Spitting image

Some African cobras do not just bite—they spit. The ringhals and the black-necked cobra are known as spitting cobras. They can send a stream of venom up to ten feet from an opening in their fangs, aiming for the enemy's eyes.

● To the Parent

Cobras belong to a family of snakes known as elapids. They are found throughout Africa, India, and Southeast Asia, and they are responsible for a number of deaths each year. The largest of them, the king cobra, can grow to 16 feet long and can lift its head six or seven feet off the ground. Cobras often live near farms, taking over mammal burrows or hiding under rocks and coming out to eat rodents.

Which Snakes Strangle Their Prey?

 ANSWER The snakes of the boa family—boa constrictors, anacondas, and pythons—are the biggest in the world. Instead of killing their prey with a bite, they squeeze it to death. When a boa sees a likely meal, such as a caiman—a relative of the alligator *(below)*—it will wait for the prey to come close. Then the boa will strike out and wrap around its prey, squeezing it until it can no longer breathe.

How often do they eat?

Boas do not use much energy, so they don't need to eat very often. When their meals are small, such as mice or lizards, they might eat every few days. But when they manage to catch a large animal, such as a caiman or a wild pig, they can go for a month or more before they eat again.

▲ **Boa Constrictor**
The boa constrictor lives in South America and grows to be about nine feet long.

▼ **Indian Python**
Pythons are boas that live in Africa, Asia, and Australia. They are good tree-climbers and often eat birds.

■ How big is a big snake?

The anaconda is the largest snake in the world. Really big anacondas may grow 20 to 30 feet long— longer than a school bus!

● **To the Parent**

The big snakes of the boa family have been associated with many lurid stories, almost all of them false. Despite the tales of 60-foot-long, man-eating boas, these snakes are in fact not dangerous to humans—and the longest one in any respectable record was 37 $\frac{1}{2}$ feet. Some people keep them as pets and have boas wrap around them without a problem.

Do Poison-Arrow Frogs Shoot Poison Arrows?

ANSWER Poison-arrow frogs live in the rain forest. These tiny frogs, no bigger than a thumb, do not shoot arrows. They have this odd name because of their poisonous skin. Even large animals do not eat them. The poison makes the animals sick. Native people from the forests capture the frogs. They dip their arrow tips in the frogs' strong poison. The poison makes each arrow a deadly weapon.

Why are these frogs so colorful?

Poison-arrow frogs come in many bright colors, including red, orange, green, blue, and yellow, often in combination with black. Their brilliant colors and bold patterns are a warning to birds, mammals, snakes, and other rain forest animals that might eat them. These animals have learned that brightly colored frogs taste terrible and may be deadly. So instead of eating the frogs, they leave them alone.

▲ Harlequin Poison Frog

▲ Green and Black Poison Frog

▲ Strawberry Poison Frog

▲ Red-Backed Poison Frog

● **To the Parent**

The poison-arrow frogs, also known as poison-dart frogs, are found in tropical rain forests of Central and South America. These brilliantly-colored amphibians secrete an extremely powerful toxin from beneath their skin that is often deadly to predators. People of certain native tribes living in the forest capture and heat the frogs to force secretion of the venom to the surface of the animals' skin. Hunters dip the tips of their arrows or darts in the liquid. The weapons then have a paralyzing effect on larger birds and mammals that the natives hunt.

Can a Bug Make You Sick?

ANSWER If a bee stings you, it hurts a lot. A mosquito bite does not hurt, but that red bump itches and itches. Stings and bites like these are minor pains. After a day or two the hurt goes away. In some parts of the world, though, an insect or tick bite can be more serious. In these places certain insects and ticks carry bacteria and viruses. A bug bite can make a person very sick in those countries.

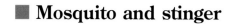

■ **Mosquito and stinger**

In most cases, when a mosquito lands on someone, that person does not even know it is there. The insect stabs the skin and drinks a little of the blood. When its meal is finished, the mosquito flies away, and the person stung has an itchy bite. Most bites are harmless, but some leave behind dangerous germs.

Which bugs carry diseases?

Many types of flies, mosquitoes, and ticks are disease carriers. Some are well-known because of a particular illness they cause. Scientists can prevent or cure some of the diseases carried by these creatures, but other diseases remain quite dangerous.

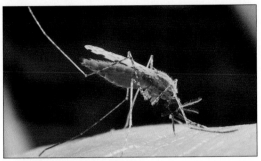

▲ *Anopheles* Mosquito

This mosquito causes a disease called malaria in parts of Africa and Asia. A person with malaria is seriously ill with a high fever.

▲ Tsetse Fly

In Africa this fly causes several illnesses, including sleeping sickness. The disease affects people and cattle.

▲ *Aedes Aegypti* Mosquito

This mosquito breeds in stagnant water, and its bite causes yellow fever. Today a vaccine protects people from this disease.

▲ Deer Tick

This tick can cause Lyme disease. For protection, people hiking through wooded areas often wear long-sleeved shirts and long pants.

■ Only females bite

Female mosquitoes need to drink animal blood to be able to lay eggs that will hatch. The males do not bite; they feed on flower nectar.

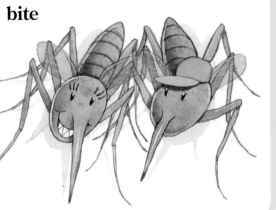

● **To the Parent**

Mosquitoes, tsetse flies, and ticks prove that some of the smallest animals are among the most dangerous ones. Some carry parasites that cause disease. Children can be taught common-sense precautions against some disease spreaders. For example, wearing long-sleeved shirts and long pants and checking for ticks after a hike can greatly reduce the risk of Lyme disease.

Can an Ant Harm You?

ANSWER Most ants you see are harmless insects. But there are a few kinds of ants that cause problems for people. One of these is the fire ant. This insect has a tiny stinger. When a fire ant climbs on a person it may sting him or her again and again. These bites are painful and can be dangerous for some people.

▲ A close-up view of fire ants.

■ Fire ant hill

Fire ants live in nests that look like mounds of soil. About 100,000 ants may live in one nest. Since the ants will attack any animal that disturbs their nest, it is best to keep away.

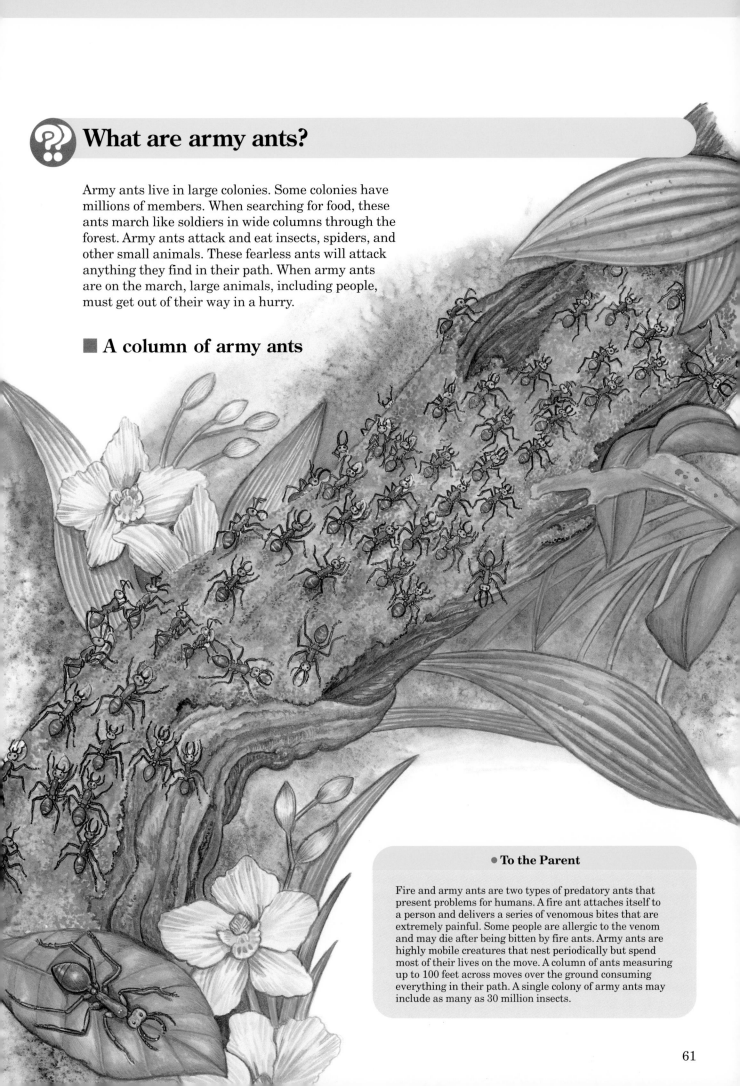

❓ What are army ants?

Army ants live in large colonies. Some colonies have millions of members. When searching for food, these ants march like soldiers in wide columns through the forest. Army ants attack and eat insects, spiders, and other small animals. These fearless ants will attack anything they find in their path. When army ants are on the march, large animals, including people, must get out of their way in a hurry.

■ **A column of army ants**

● **To the Parent**

Fire and army ants are two types of predatory ants that present problems for humans. A fire ant attaches itself to a person and delivers a series of venomous bites that are extremely painful. Some people are allergic to the venom and may die after being bitten by fire ants. Army ants are highly mobile creatures that nest periodically but spend most of their lives on the move. A column of ants measuring up to 100 feet across moves over the ground consuming everything in their path. A single colony of army ants may include as many as 30 million insects.

What Are Killer Bees?

ANSWER Killer bees are a type of wild honey-bee. They live in places where the weather is warm. Like all honeybees, a killer bee stings when someone bothers it. The strange thing is, these bees act as if they are angrier than other types. Large groups of these bees will swarm around a person and sting. Because they attack with such force, people call them "killer bees."

▲ **A killer bee** *(left)* **is smaller than a honeybee.**

■ Bee keeper

Bee keepers cover up every part of their body to keep from getting stung while collecting honey from their hives. They worry about killer bees joining their hives.

■ Wild hive

Killer bees live in nests like this one. They travel greater distances than other bees to start new nests. But sometimes they move into bee keepers' hives.

What can we do about killer bees?

Unfortunately, there is nothing we can do to stop these insects. Killer bees first got loose in South America about 40 years ago and have been spreading ever since. The map on the right shows how the bees got to the United States from Mexico. Over time they will settle in many parts of the southern United States. People in these areas will have to learn to be careful around bees.

■ Studying bees

Scientists are tracking the spread of killer bees. They use special equipment to trap and compare bees. In time they may discover ways to stop their advance or make them less dangerous.

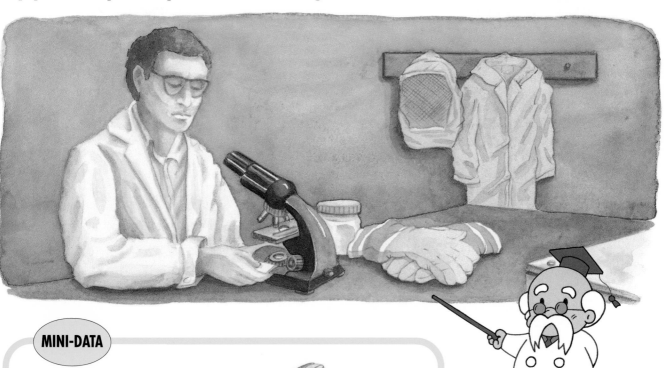

■ Bees at work

In spite of their sting, all honeybees, including killer bees, are an important part of nature. As they go from flower to flower, they pick up grains of yellow pollen on their bodies and legs. This spreads the pollen around and helps flowers and blossoms develop seeds and fruits.

● **To the Parent**

In 1956 African bees were brought to Brazil in an effort to improve honey production. When some queen bees were accidentally released they mated with indigenous bees to produce the strain known as killer bees. The bees have displaced more docile populations and spread out from Brazil. They arrived in Texas in 1990 and will soon nest in much of the south.

How Did the Black Widow Spider Get Its Name?

ANSWER A female black widow spins a web that becomes her home. This is where she raises her spiderlings. Sometimes, when a male comes to the web, the female eats the male. The female is black with a red mark in the shape of an hourglass on her abdomen. Women who have lost their husbands are known as widows. Since this spider often loses her mate, people call her the "black widow" spider.

■ Spider life

A black widow lives in her web. Here she waits for a mate and catches insects for food. When a spider bites, it injects a poisonous venom. The female black widow has one of the strongest venoms of any spider. It is poisonous enough to harm people.

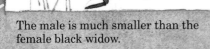

The male is much smaller than the female black widow.

64

Are there other dangerous spiders?

The hairy tarantula is the largest of all spiders. The body can be as long as 3½ inches and the legs extend to ten inches, which is larger than a man's hand. Tarantulas feed on frogs, lizards, mice, and insects, and sometimes even birds. They attack their prey with a poisonous bite, but they do not harm people.

■ Scary scorpions

Scorpions are relatives of spiders. These hunters sting their prey with their poisonous tails. Many scorpions live in the desert where they hunt small creatures such as insects and spiders. A person out walking in the evening may not see the scorpion and get stung by accident. A scorpion sting should be treated by a doctor.

Do Jellyfish Have Jelly Inside?

ANSWER A jellyfish floats in the ocean. Most of its clear body is filled with gas or water that wiggles like jelly. This animal looks harmless, but it is not. The hanging arms, called tentacles, are covered with stinging threads. When a fish swims by, the jellyfish shoots its stingers into it. The sting stuns the fish, and the jellyfish can grab the fish with its tentacles and eat it.

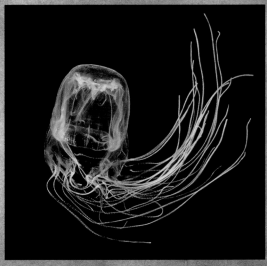

The sea wasp from the South Pacific stings with a deadly poison from 33-foot-long tentacles.

■ **A swimming jellyfish**

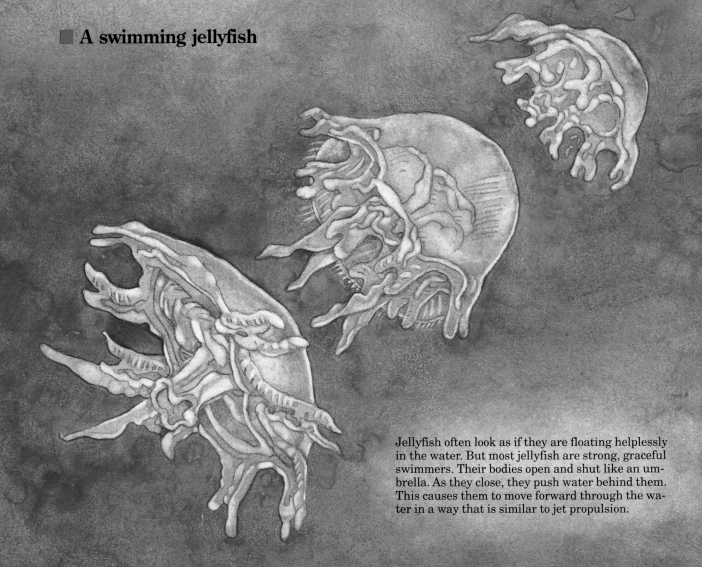

Jellyfish often look as if they are floating helplessly in the water. But most jellyfish are strong, graceful swimmers. Their bodies open and shut like an umbrella. As they close, they push water behind them. This causes them to move forward through the water in a way that is similar to jet propulsion.

Is a Portuguese man-of-war a jellyfish?

The Portuguese man-of-war is not a true jellyfish. It is a colony of animals living together. Floating on top of the water is a gas-filled bag that acts like a sail in the wind. Below the water are long tentacles clinging to the bag, each an animal of its own. The jellyfish's funny name comes from the saillike bag. It looks like an old sailing ship called a Portuguese man-of-war.

Stinging tentacles

The tentacles' poisonous sting kills small fish. The food is then shared by all the animals in the colony.

● **To the Parent**

True jellyfish and the Portuguese man-of-war belong to the phylum of coelenterates. A jellyfish gets its name from the gelatinous material called mesoglea that makes up part of its body. Swimmers should stay away from jellyfish, even those that have died and washed up on shore. Some jellyfish have venomous stingers that remain active after the death of the animal.

How Does the Hammerhead Shark Use Its Head?

ANSWER Hammerhead is the perfect name for this shark. Its head is shaped like the top of a hammer. This strange-looking head helps the shark make quick turns in the water. That's why it is known as a deadly hunter. The hammerhead is a dangerous shark. It hunts large fish, and sometimes it attacks people.

■ **Dangerous to humans**

Tiger Shark

Great White Shark

Hammerhead Shark

Are all Sharks Dangerous?

Many people are afraid of sharks. They tell frightening stories of sharks attacking divers and swimmers. In truth, though, most sharks never harm people. Only a few types, including the hammerhead, great white shark, and tiger shark, can be deadly. The largest and scariest-looking shark of all, known as the whale shark, grows to an enormous length of 45 feet, but it poses no danger to people. Whale sharks have no teeth, and they feed on plankton, squid, and tiny fish. The smallest shark is the dwarf shark; it is only six inches long and harmless.

■ Harmless sharks

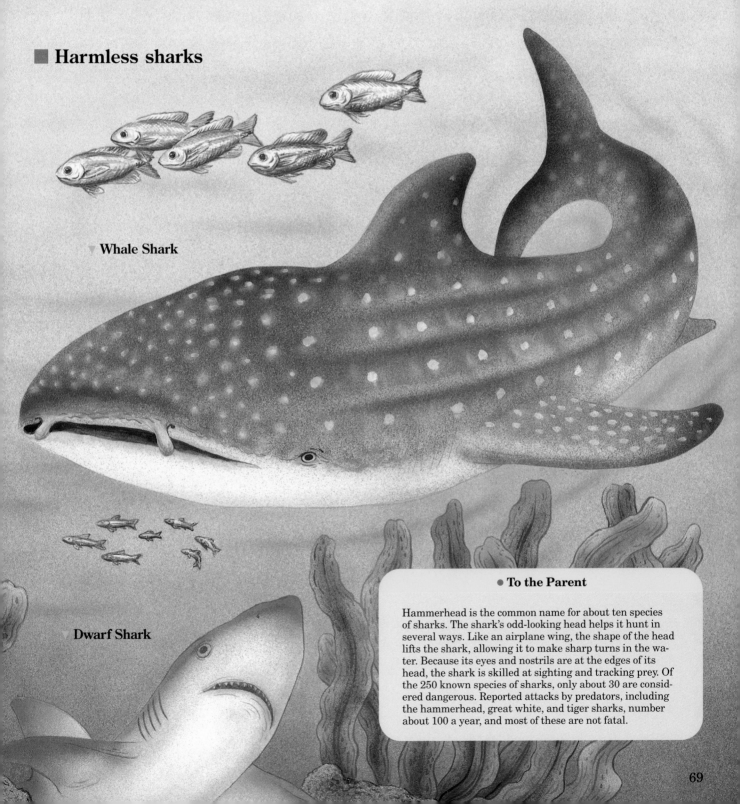

▼ Whale Shark

Dwarf Shark

● **To the Parent**

Hammerhead is the common name for about ten species of sharks. The shark's odd-looking head helps it hunt in several ways. Like an airplane wing, the shape of the head lifts the shark, allowing it to make sharp turns in the water. Because its eyes and nostrils are at the edges of its head, the shark is skilled at sighting and tracking prey. Of the 250 known species of sharks, only about 30 are considered dangerous. Reported attacks by predators, including the hammerhead, great white, and tiger sharks, number about 100 a year, and most of these are not fatal.

How Does a Swordfish Use Its Sword?

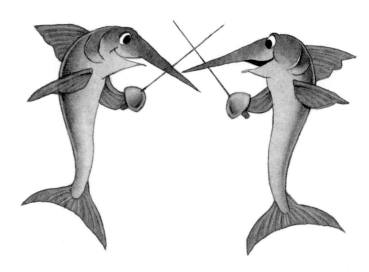

ANSWER The swordfish's sword is a long, bony piece coming out of its head. The sword is not sharp, but it is very useful. Like a belly-board for floating in the ocean, the sword helps the fish cut through the water. That makes the swordfish one of the fastest swimmers in the sea. The sword-fish also uses its sword to attack and catch smaller fish.

Sometimes the sword works as a weapon. When a swordfish swims through a school of fish, it slashes at the water. Some of the smaller fish are hit by the sword and injured. Before they can escape, the swordfish eats them.

Do other sea creatures have swords?

Some other fish, the marlin, for example, have snouts that look like a swordfish's sword. The sawfish and the narwhal have different kinds of "swords." Each animal's sword is designed to help it survive in the ocean.

▼ **Sawfish**

The sawfish has sawlike teeth on the sides of its snout. The teeth do great damage when the sawfish slashes at schools of fish. The saw also helps to dig up shellfish from the ocean floor.

▶ **Blue Marlin**

The marlin's sword looks like the swordfish's, but its snout is shorter and rounded at the end. This fast-swimming fish uses its weapon much the way a swordfish does.

▲ **Narwhal**

The narwhal is not a fish; it is a strange-looking whale. Male narwhals have a tusk that grows into a sharp, long spiral. The male may use its tusk to fight with other males.

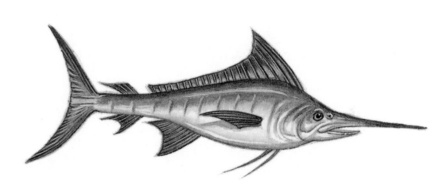

How Did the Killer Whale Get Its Name?

ANSWER The killer whale is a popular animal. People love to watch this graceful whale in an aquarium or marine park. In the ocean, the whale's main job is to search for its food. It hunts many animals, including fish, seals, penguins, and other kinds of whales that are much larger than it. That is why it is known as a killer whale.

■ **Little ones against the big one**

Killer whales often travel and hunt in groups called pods. In a pod of as many as 30, killer whales will even attack the blue whale—the largest animal of all. No wonder killer whales are known as the greatest hunters in the ocean.

How do people train killer whales?

In places like Sea World, trainers develop a close relationship with killer whales. By feeding them, "playing" with them, and helping to take care of them, the staff can train the whales to do things that come naturally, but look like difficult acts.

▼ During a performance at Sea World, killer whales delight the crowd with great leaps out of the water.

▼ After the performance, a killer whale greets a young visitor.

▲ At the end of a performance, the whales swim to the edge of the pool to be rewarded by their trainers, as here with handfuls of small fish.

● **To the Parent**

The killer whale is a skillful hunter. Although its main diet is fish, killer whales feed on many sea creatures, including other mammals. Armed with teeth for grasping, the 16- to 22-foot-long whales can swallow animals such as seals in one big gulp. Killer whales do not prey on people.

Which Sea Creature Harms the Most People?

ANSWER You might think the shark is the most dangerous creature in the sea, but it is not. Stingray wounds are much more common than shark bites. Stingrays are fish with long whiplike tails.

They rest on the ocean floor hidden in the sand. When a person steps on a stingray, it snaps its tail to defend itself. The tail will latch onto the intruder and deliver a painful sting.

A swimming stingray is easy to see. When it rests on the ocean floor, it is hard to find. The color and pattern of its skin help it blend in with the sand. When a person steps on a stingray, it stings with its sharp tail.

Do all rays sting?

All rays have tails, though in some types they are quite small. Most rays use their tails the way a ship uses a rudder to steer through the water. Only certain ones use their barbed tails as weapons, and not all of them are poisonous.

▲ **Manta Ray**
This scary-looking ray measures up to 20 feet across, but it is harmless. It feeds on tiny sea creatures that it funnels into its mouth with its front fins.

■ **How they sting**

A stingray's tail has tiny hooklike teeth that stick in a person's leg. Sometimes the sting is both painful and poisonous.

● **To the Parent**

Rays are cartilaginous fish that are close relatives of the sharks. Stingrays have developed tails as defensive weapons. When stepped on, a stingray whips its barbed tail onto the intruder with painful results. Often the tail breaks off and remains imbedded in the wound. Some stingrays are venomous, adding to the danger for unsuspecting bathers.

What Is the Most Poisonous Fish in the World?

(ANSWER) The stonefish of the South Pacific has the strongest poison of all. This fish looks like a seaweed-covered stone. When it rests on the rocky ocean floor it is almost impossible to see. The spines on the stonefish's back deliver a powerful shot of poison. A person stepping on the spines will be seriously injured.

The stonefish hides among rocks and coral reefs. Tiny fish do not know there is a hunter waiting until it is too late. The stonefish swallows its meal with one quick gulp. The deadly spines on its back protect the fish from other predators.

What are some other poisonous fish?

The stonefish is a member of the scorpionfish family. Some fish in this family also have venomous spines but are not as deadly. They include the lionfish and the turkeyfish. Other poisonous fish include the weeverfish and certain puffers.

▲ **Lionfish**
Instead of hiding in the rocks, this relative of the stonefish shows off its beautiful colors. Each feathery spine is really a poisonous weapon.

▲ **Pufferfish**
The pufferfish's way to scare the enemy away is by puffing itself up to more than twice its size. It grows so large that other fish cannot eat it. Some of them are poisonous, too. A fish that eats one gets a deadly meal.

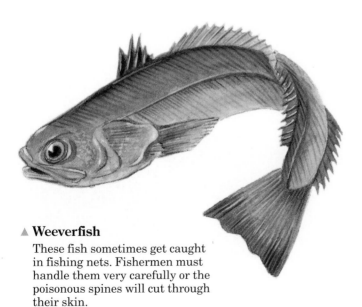

▲ **Weeverfish**
These fish sometimes get caught in fishing nets. Fishermen must handle them very carefully or the poisonous spines will cut through their skin.

● **To the Parent**

The stonefish is a member of the scorpionfish family, which includes many other fish with venomous spines. One of the most beautiful of these is the lionfish, which swims in warm water near coral reefs. The weeverfish is a different type of venomous fish, found in cooler waters. Pufferfish do not sting, but some contain a powerful poison in their internal organs.

Which Animals Are Not as Dangerous as They Look?

ANSWER Dangerous animals are often easy to spot. Many of them have bright colors. Their colors warn others to keep away. Some animals copy the way dangerous animals look; this look is called mimicry. These copycats are harmless. They trick other animals into leaving them alone.

▲ **Snake or what?**

This looks like the head of the poisonous palm viper but it isn't a snake at all. It is the silk moth caterpillar mimicking a snake.

■ Look-alike snakes

A rhyme to remember the poisonous one

Red touch yellow, could hurt a fellow.
Red touch black, won't hurt Jack.

▲ **Coral Snake**

This family of aggressive snakes is highly poisonous. A coral snake is easily recognized by the pattern of red, yellow, and black stripes on its skin.

▲ **Kingsnake**

The harmless kingsnake has the same striped colors as a coral snake. Animals that might otherwise eat the kingsnake think it is dangerous and stay away.

Which of these really do sting?

If you are not careful, a bee or yellow jacket will sting you. These insects are often recognized by their striped bodies. Many harmless insects copy this pattern of colors. Some use additional tricks. The hoverfly flaps its wings to make a sound just like a buzzing bee.

▲ **Wasp Beetle**
This is a harmless beetle, not a stinging wasp.

◀ **Yellow Jacket**
This wasp inflicts a painful sting.

▲ **Honeybee**
A bee will sting when it is disturbed.

▲ **Clearwing Moth**
Its clear wings make it look like a stinging insect.

◀ **Striped Drone Fly**
Its striped pattern makes it seem dangerous.

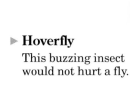

▶ **Hoverfly**
This buzzing insect would not hurt a fly.

● **To the Parent**

Bright colors and bold patterns serve as a warning in nature. Often venomous or stinging animals advertise their dangerous attributes, and many species of predators learn to keep their distance. For other harmless animals, mimicry has developed as an effective defense. Disguised to look like a dangerous animal, these imitators "hide" while in plain sight.

What Is the Most Dangerous Animal?

ANSWER The most dangerous animal is not the lion or grizzly bear. It is not the great white shark or killer bee. If you want to see it, take a look in the mirror. People are the most dangerous animals.

■ Clearing the land

As people clear forests to make room for homes and farms, they destroy animals' homes and the food they eat. Without a place to live, many animals die.

■ Dangerous chemicals

People spray pesticides on fields to kill harmful insects. The insects die, but the poison is flushed into rivers, where it kills fish, water birds, and other animals.

■ Illegal hunting

Poachers, hunting illegally, have recklessly killed certain rare animals, such as leopards for their furs and elephants for their tusks. These animals are now in danger of becoming extinct.

● **To the Parent**

Poaching, habitat destruction, and the use of pesticides are some of the ways people place their fellow animals at risk. These complex issues are difficult for children to comprehend, but children can be encouraged to respect all living things.

Growing-Up Album

Whose Antlers Are These?

The deer, elk, and moose pictured below need your help.
They have lost their antlers. Can you match the antlers
to each animal?

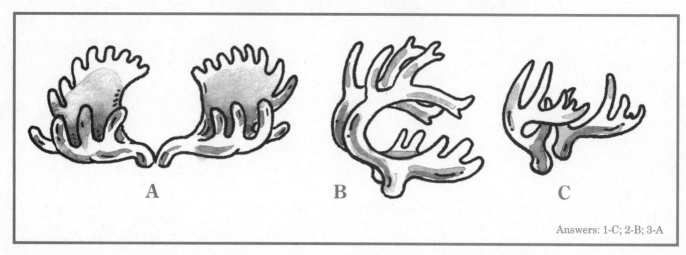

A   B   C

Whose Horns Are These?

The rhinocerus, Cape buffalo, and bison look really strange without their horns. Can you find the right horns belonging to each animal?

1 ☐

2 ☐

3 ☐

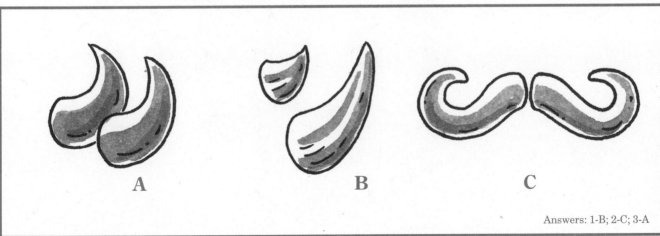

A   B   C

Answers: 1-B; 2-C; 3-A

83

Why Are These Animals Dangerous?

Dangerous animals have all kinds of weapons to protect themselves. Can you name the weapons these animals use?

1. _____

2. _____

3. _____

4. _____

5. _____

6. _____

7. _____

8. _____

9. _____

10. _____

11. _____

Answers: 1-Bear: teeth and claws. 2-Moose: hooves and antlers. 3-Poison arrow frog: poisonous skin. 4-Anaconda: stranglehold. 5-Bee: stinger. 6-Wolf: teeth. 7.-Cobra: fangs. 8-Crocodile: teeth and jaws. 9-Jaguar: teeth and claws. 10-Sea wasp jellyfish: stinging tentacles. 11-Cassowary: spurs.

Where Do They Live?

Dangerous animals live in many different environments. Can you tell which area each of these animals is from? Match each animal with its natural home.

A. Desert

1. Sea Wasp

2. Wolf

3. Lion

7. Elephant

8. Rattlesnake

9. Alligator

C. Northern forests

B. Grasslands

4. Moose

5. Gila Monster

6. Shark

10. Scorpion

11. Bear

12. Cape Buffalo

D. Coastal waters

Time-Life Books is a division of Time Life Inc.

TIME LIFE INC.

PRESIDENT and CEO: George Artandi

TIME-LIFE BOOKS

PRESIDENT: John D. Hall
PUBLISHER/MANAGING EDITOR: Neil Kagan

A Child's First Library of Learning
DANGEROUS ANIMALS

EDITOR: Karin Kinney
DIRECTOR, NEW PRODUCT DEVELOPMENT: Elizabeth D. Ward
MARKETING DIRECTOR: Wendy A. Foster

Marketing Manager: Janine Wilkin
Picture Coordinator: David A. Herod
Picture Researcher (Intern): Kristen Desmond
Editorial Assistant: Mary Saxton

Design: Studio A—Antonio Alcalá, Sue Dowdall, Virginia Ibarra-Garza,
Wendy Schleicher, Melissa Wilets
Special Contributors: Patricia Daniels, Kristen Desmond (Intern), An-
drew Gutelle, Jocelyn Lindsay (Research and Writing)
Consultant: George E. Watson is the former curator of birds and chair-
man of the Department of Vertebrate Zoology in the Smithsonian Institu-
tion's National Museum of Natural History.
Correspondents: Maria Vincenza Aloisi (Paris), Christine Hinze
(London), Christina Lieberman (New York).

Vice President, Director of Finance: Christopher Hearing
Vice President, Book Production: Marjann Caldwell
Director of Operations: Eileen Bradley
Director of Photography and Research: John Conrad Weiser
Director of Editorial Administration (Acting): Barbara Levitt
Production Manager: Marlene Zack
Quality Assurance Manager: James King
Library: Louise D. Forstall

Photography: Cover: © 1994 Joseph Van Os/The Image Bank. Back Cover: Images
© 1996 PhotoDisc, Inc. 1: Images © 1996 PhotoDisc, Inc. 10: © Eberhard Brunner,
Photographers/Aspen, Inc. 11: Peter Davey/Bruce Coleman Limited, Uxbridge,
Middlesex. 14: Aberham/IFA-Bilderteam, Munich. 16: Images © 1996 PhotoDisc,
Inc. 17: © S. Prude Matthews/Tony Stone Images. 19: (c) Dani-Jeske/Animals Ani-
mals. 22: Dimitri Kessel for LIFE. 23: © Renee Lynn/Tony Stone Images; © Tim
Davis/Tony Stone Images–San Diego Museum of Man/Mr. and Mrs. Albert
Gildred Collection. 24: © David Hiser, Photographers/Aspen, Inc.— ©Peter
Weimann/Animals Animals. 27: © Nicholas DeVore/Tony Stone Images. 30: © Dan
Guravich. 31: © Art Wolfe/Tony Stone Images. 33: © Ray Richardson/Animals Ani-
mals. 34: Silvestris, Kastl, Germany. 35: © Ederegger/Peter Arnold, Inc.; Images ©
1996 PhotoDisc, Inc. 36: Images © 1996 PhotoDisc. 38, 39: Merlin D. Tuttle,
BAT Conservation International. 44: © Rudie Kuiter/Oxford Scientific Films, Long
Hanborough, Oxfordshire; © Whit Bronaugh; © Mike Bacon/Tom Stack & Associ-
ates. 45: © 1996, D. Cavagnaro/DRK Photo; Neville Coleman/Planet Earth Pic-
tures, London. 46: © 1996, John Cancalosi/DRK Photo. 47: S.C. Bisserot/Nature
Photographers Limited, Tadley, Hampshire. 48: Tony Stone Bilderwelten, Munich.
49: E. & D. Hosking/FLPA Limited, Suffolk; © Michael Fogden/Bruce Coleman,
Inc. 50: © Ed Robinson/Tom Stack & Associates. 53: © 1996, Michael Fogden/DRK
Photo. 54: © Wolfgang Bayer/Bruce Coleman, Inc. 55: © 1996, John Cancalosi/
DRK Photo; Cris Crowley/Tom Stack & Associates. 59: Tim Shepherd/Oxford Sci-
entific Films, Long Hanborough, Oxfordshire; J.A.L. Cooke/Oxford Scientific
Films, Long Hanborough, Oxfordshire (2); J.A. Grant/Natural Science Photos, Wat-
ford, Hertfordshire. 60: Ester Beaton/Planet Earth Pictures, London. 62: Agricultur-
al Research Service, USDA. 65: © 1996, James P. Rowan/DRK Photo. 66: Neville
Coleman/Planet Earth Pictures, London. 67: Peter Scoones/Planet Earth Pictures,

London. 73: Courtesy Sea World, Inc. 75: Maza/Jacana, Paris. 76: Hal Beral/Natural
Science Photos, Watford, Hertfordshire. 78: David M. Dennis/Tom Stack & Associates. 79: Photos clockwise starting at top left: © K.G. Vock/Okapia/Oxford Scientific Films, Long Hanborough, Oxfordshire; © E.R. Degginger/Animals Animals; ©
Bill Ivy/Tony Stone Images; © Donald Specker/Animals Animals; John Mason/
Ardea Limited, London; B. Borrell/FLPA Limited, Stowmarket, Suffolk. 81: Images
© 1996 PhotoDisc, Inc.

Illustrations: Loel Barr: 9 (lower left), 13 (top), 19 (top), 25 (top), 28 (top), 32 (top),
35, 40 (middle), 47 (top), 54 (top), 55 (bottom), 82-87; Robin DeWitt: 13 (bottom left
and right), 20-21, 28 (bottom), 29 (top), 34, 37 (bottom), 40 (bottom), 41, 60-61, 71;
Al Kettler: 63; Annie Lunsford: 15 (bottom), 23, 30-31, 37 (top), 40 (top), 58 (top), 59,
64 (top), 68 (top), 70; Lili Robins: 14, 15 (top left and right), 16-17, 25 (middle), 42, 43
(middle and bottom), 49, 62, 63 (middle and bottom), 72 (bottom), 76-77; Carol
Schwartz: 4-5, 6-7, 8, 9 (lower right), 12, 18 (bottom), 19 (bottom), 22, 44-45, 53, 56-
57, 58 (bottom), 68-69, 74-75, 78; Bethann Thornburgh: 11 (bottom), 16 (top), 18
(top), 24, 29 (bottom), 32 (bottom), 33, 39, 43 (top), 47 (bottom), 50 (bottom), 51
(top), 52, 55, 72 (top); Bobbi Tull: 9, 10, 11 (top), 26-27, 46, 50 (middle), 51 (middle
and bottom), 64 (middle and bottom), 65, 66-67, 80; Stephen Wagner: cover.

First printing. Printed in U.S.A.
School and library distribution by Time-Life Education, P.O. Box 85026,
Richmond, Virginia 23285-5026.

Time Life is a trademark of Time Warner Inc. U.S.A.

Library of Congress Cataloging-in-Publication Data
Dangerous animals.
    88 p. cm.—(A Child's First Library of Learning)
    Summary: Uses a question-and-answer format to present information
about some of the ways various animals protect themselves.
    ISBN 0-8094-9480-9
    1. Dangerous animals—Miscellanea—Juvenile literature. [1. Animal
defenses–Miscellanea. 2. Animal weapons—Miscellanea. 3. Questions
and answers.] I. Time-Life Books. II. Series.
QL100.D35 1996
591.6'5—dc20   96-32941
                                    CIP
                                    AC

OTHER PUBLICATIONS

COOKING	DO IT YOURSELF
Weight Watchers®, Smart Choice	The Time-Life Complete Gardener
Recipe Collection	Home Repair and Improvement
Great Taste–Low Fat	The Art of Woodworking
Williams-Sonoma Kitchen Library	Fix It Yourself

TIME-LIFE KIDS	HISTORY
Family Time Bible Stories	The American Story
Library of First Questions and Answers	Voices of the Civil War
A Child's First Library of Learning	The American Indians
I Love Math	Lost Civilizations
Nature Company Discoveries	Mysteries of the Unknown
Understanding Science & Nature	Time Frame
	The Civil War
SCIENCE/NATURE	Cultural Atlas
Voyage Through the Universe	

For information on and a full description of any of the Time-Life Books
series listed above, please call 1-800-621-7026 or write:

Reader Information
Time-Life Customer Service
P.O. Box C-32068
Richmond, Virginia 23261-2068